Alex Karp

ALEX KARP

The Philosopher CEO

Debra C. Lee

Alex Karp

All rights reserved. No part of this publication may be reproduced, distributed, or transmitted in any form or by any means, including photocopying, recording, or other electronic or mechanical method, without the prior written permission of the publisher, except in the case of brief quotations embodied in critical reviews and certain other noncommercial uses permitted by the copyright law.
Copyright © Debra C. Lee, 2024.

Alex Karp

TABLE OF CONTENTS

INTRODUCTION

CHAPTER 1: WHO IS ALEX KARP

Childhood and early years

Path of Study

CHAPTER 2: THE PATH TO PALANTIR

Getting to know Peter Thiel

Palantir Technologies' Inception

Academic Contributions and Dissertations

First Difficulties and Achievements

CHAPTER 3. LEADERSHIP AND PHILOSOPHY IN BUSINESS

The CEO of Philosopher

The Leadership Style of Karp

Organizational Culture

Palantir's values and ethics

Handling Differing Opinions

Handling Public and Political Scrutiny

CHAPTER 4: GROWTH AND EXPANSION

Palantir's Worldwide Impact

Prospective Courses

CONCLUSION

Alex Karp

INTRODUCTION

Few individuals in the rapidly evolving area of technology are as unique as Alex Karp, the enigmatic CEO and co-founder of Palantir Technologies. While many IT leaders hold degrees in business or engineering, Karp's journey to becoming the head of one of the biggest data analytics companies in the world began in the humanities and is notable for its unique combination of entrepreneurial fervor and philosophical exploration.

In his early years, Karp was highly curious about the world of ideas. His family encouraged both scientific rigor and creative imagination, and he was born and raised in New York City. Based on this, he pursued a diverse academic career, earning a Ph.D. in neoclassical social theory from Goethe University in Frankfurt, Germany, a bachelor's degree from Haverford College, and a J.D. from Stanford Law School. Karp's varied educational background set him apart from his peers and gave his economic acumen a distinct philosophical perspective.

"Alex Karp: The Philosopher CEO" delves into the biography of an exceptional business tycoon, demonstrating how his scholarly pursuits and intense intellectual curiosity molded both his vision for Palantir and his leadership approach. From his early fascination with the complexities of human society to his groundbreaking work in big data analytics, Karp's biography is one of unwavering curiosity, inventive thinking, and a determination to tackle some of the most significant issues facing the globe.

In this book, Karp's journey from his early years in New York to the power corridors of Silicon Valley is chronicled. There, he successfully navigates the difficulties of building a company that integrates technology and social impact. It examines how he contributed to making Palantir an essential tool for commercial and governmental entities around the world,

Alex Karp

covering everything from counterterrorism to healthcare analytics.

"Alex Karp: The Philosopher CEO" provides readers with an in-depth understanding of the man behind Palantir with candid interviews, exclusive behind-the-scenes knowledge, and a thorough examination of his career and personal experiences. It sheds light on his innovative use of data and technology, his philosophical underpinnings, and his dedication to creating tools that promote transparency and moral decision-making in addition to increasing productivity.

As you read this book, you will gain more knowledge about how Alex Karp's unique leadership style and philosophy shaped his career and continues to influence the IT industry. His story is an ode to the merits of unconventional thinking and the concord that arises from marrying intellectual integrity with business ambition. From the world of CEO and philosopher Alex Karp, who is revolutionizing the application of data analytics and technology, greetings.

Alex Karp

CHAPTER 1: WHO IS ALEX KARP

The CEO and co-founder of Palantir Technologies, a publicly traded software company that specializes in big data analytics, is American businessman Alex Karp. Founded in 2003 by Peter Thiel and other investors, Palantir is a software firm that focuses on offering large-scale data integration, analysis, and visualization solutions to major corporations and government agencies.

Graduates of Goethe University in Frankfurt, Germany, Haverford College, Stanford Law School, and neoclassical social theory Ph.D. recipient Karp is a graduate of all three institutions. Karp doesn't have a traditional IT background, but he has been instrumental in driving Palantir's growth and maintaining its inventive, clandestine culture.

Alex Karp

Under Karp's leadership, Palantir has made a substantial contribution to a variety of high-profile projects, including government counterterrorism operations and commercial data analysis projects. Karp is still a well-known figure in the business and technology sectors, respected for his frank and unconventional opinions on privacy, data security, and the role of the IT industry in society.

Childhood and early years

Alex Karp's early years and upbringing provide an interesting backdrop for his success as a technology entrepreneur and CEO of Palantir Technologies. Karp grew up in a household that valued intellectual curiosity as well as diversity of ethnicity. On October 2, 1967, in New York City, he was born. Because his father was a pediatrician and his mother was an artist, he was exposed to science, medicine, and the arts from an early age.

Alex Karp

Karp's liberal, intellectual upbringing had a significant impact on the way he thought. His parents encouraged critical thinking and an open mind, which pushed him towards independence and intellectual rigor. Growing up in a city as culturally diverse as New York, Karp was exposed to a wide range of educational and cultural possibilities, which fueled his curiosity and quest for knowledge.

Karp had a successful academic career from the beginning. At Central High School in Philadelphia, he excelled academically. His interest in a variety of areas, such as philosophy and physics, was evident even in school. This ability to be conceptually flexible would later come to characterize his career.

Karp's development was also greatly influenced by his background. His father, a pediatrician, instilled in him discipline and a methodical approach to problem-solving. His mother, an artist, fostered his creative side by teaching him to appreciate unconventional perspectives and think imaginatively.

Alex Karp

This fusion of scientific rigor and creative thinking would later come to define Karp's leadership style at Palantir.

After high school, Karp continued his education with the same spirit of intellectual curiosity that had defined his formative years. He was a student at the liberal arts school Haverford College, which is well-known for its challenging curriculum and focus on social responsibility. Karp attended Haverford College to pursue a comprehensive education, eventually earning a bachelor's degree there. His time at Haverford enhanced his commitment to intellectual curiosity and social impact, two things that would later guide his work at Palantir.

Following his graduation from Haverford, Karp pursued further education. Later, Karp earned his J.D. from Stanford Law School, one of the most prestigious legal schools in the nation. It was during his time at Stanford that his interests began to shift toward the intersection of law, technology, and society. His interest in how legal

Alex Karp

systems might respond to emerging technologies developed.

After leaving Stanford, Karp went to Goethe University in Frankfurt, Germany, to finish his doctorate in neoclassical social theory. While this may seem a bit unusual for a would-be software entrepreneur, it does demonstrate Karp's commitment to thorough research. His dissertation research, which focused on the philosophical and social implications of economic and technical systems, gave him a unique perspective on the role of technology in society.

When Karp was in Germany, he immersed himself in the intellectual and cultural milieu of the region. He made a name for himself as an independent, analytical thinker who wasn't afraid to challenge conventional thought. He was also exposed to the broader European tradition of thought at this period of his life, which improved his education in America and expanded his viewpoint.

Alex Karp

Karp's background in social philosophy, law, and liberal arts provided him with a solid foundation for his work at Palantir. It endowed him with a unique set of skills and perspectives that enabled him to successfully navigate the complex relationships that exist between the law, society, and technology.

In conclusion, Alex Karp's early life and upbringing were marked by a commitment to individual thought, diversity in culture, and intellectual curiosity. His early exposure to demanding academics, the arts, and science equipped him with the skills he needed to succeed as a digital entrepreneur. After graduating from prestigious universities such as Haverford, Stanford, and Goethe University and moving to the intellectually and culturally rich city of New York City, Karp acquired the skills necessary to lead Palantir Technologies in its mission to use big data for societal good.

Path of Study

Alex Karp

Alex Karp's scholastic journey is a fascinating blend of intense study and intellectual exploration, deeply rooted in his enthusiasm for philosophy. Early curiosity in the theoretical underpinnings of human behavior and cognition would have a lasting impact on Karp's academic and professional endeavors.

Karp began his undergraduate studies at Haverford College, a liberal arts college known for promoting ethical reasoning and critical thinking. Karp was active in the intellectual community at Haverford in addition to being a stellar student. Despite studying many other courses, philosophy was the one that truly piqued his interest. Karp's hard studies in metaphysics, philosophy of mind, and ethical theory laid a strong basis for his subsequent academic pursuits.

Karp went overseas after earning his bachelor's degree in an attempt to broaden his horizons. He enrolled at the prestigious Goethe University in Frankfurt, Germany, which is well-known for its lengthy tradition in critical theory and philosophy. During this period, Karp read a

Alex Karp

lot of European philosophers' writings, particularly those of the Frankfurt School, which emphasized the need for critical theory in understanding culture and society. This was a pivotal period in Karp's life since it exposed him to a wide range of philosophical stances and deepened his comprehension of the complexities of human civilization.

The apex of Karp's academic career was his pursuit of a doctorate in philosophy at Stanford University. At Stanford, he received mentoring from some of the most distinguished philosophers in the field. His dissertation thesis, which focused on the intersection of philosophy, law, and ethics, demonstrated his long-standing interest in applying philosophical concepts to real-world issues. Karp's dissertation explored the ethical implications of surveillance and privacy, a topic he would later find to be crucial to his work at Palantir Technologies.

Throughout his academic career, Karp was known for his strong interest and meticulous study. Rather than merely analyzing contemporary situations, he sought to close the

Alex Karp

gap between theory and practice by applying philosophical ideas to them. This approach was evident in his academic writings, which often addressed significant societal and ethical concerns.

Karp's achievements in the classroom were matched by his commitment to the intellectual community. He attended a considerable quantity of lectures, conferences, and debates, regularly contributing to the greater philosophical discourse by presenting remarks. His instructors and classmates saw him as a thoughtful, innovative thinker who wasn't afraid to push the boundaries and challenge conventional wisdom.

Alex Karp

CHAPTER 2: THE PATH TO PALANTIR

Through a series of fortunate meetings, inspiring ideas, and unwavering dedication to using technology for social benefit, Alex Karp founded Palantir Technologies. Karp pursued a variety of academic and professional endeavours to obtain important expertise and insight before starting his own business.

Karp's first foray into the corporate world came through a succession of consulting and advising positions following his graduation from college. Because of these early encounters, he was able to see the real-world implications of his philosophical education and became very interested in the use of technology to solve challenging issues. Karp immediately distinguished himself in the business sphere with his special fusion of pragmatic understanding and philosophical insight.

Karp got to know prominent investor and entrepreneur Peter Thiel during this time, who is most known for

Alex Karp

helping to co-found PayPal. Thiel was drawn to Karp's nontraditional method of problem-solving as they both had an interest in philosophy and technology. The two became close intellectual friends, often delving deeply into topics such as the moral implications of technology and the potential for data to influence social change. The foundation for the establishment of Palantir Technologies was created by this intellectual collaboration. Motivated by their common goal, Nathan Gettings, Joe Lonsdale, Stephen Cohen, and Thiel set out to establish a business that would use cutting-edge data analysis to address some of the most important problems facing the modern world. Their objective was to develop a platform that could combine and analyze enormous volumes of data and offer insightful information to businesses in a variety of industries.

Ambition and uncertainty were mixed in Palantir's early days. Karp and his group had to overcome many obstacles, such as finding finance and creating a strong technology foundation. Nonetheless, they remained focused because of their unshakable dedication to their

Alex Karp

goal. Karp in particular was instrumental in developing the company's mission and core principles by highlighting the moral implications of their work as well as the value of civil liberties and privacy.

Gaining potential clients' trust was one of Palantir's early challenges. Regarding the nascent company's potential and the ramifications of its technology, several organizations had doubts. Karp and his group committed to showcasing the benefits and security of their platform to get past this. They collaborated actively with early adopters, demonstrating the potential of their technology through fruitful trial projects and improving it in response to feedback.

Palantir achieved significant success by obtaining contracts from multiple government organizations, such as the Department of Defence and the CIA. These agreements gave Palantir the resources it needed to grow its skills and reach while also validating its technology. Palantir started to gain a reputation for providing potent

Alex Karp

data analysis capabilities that could handle important national security concerns under Karp's direction. Karp kept stressing the value of ethical considerations in their work even as Palantir expanded. In his view, technology should not be used to restrict personal freedoms but rather to improve accountability and openness. Palantir stood apart from other tech companies thanks to its ethical position, which also drew in customers who had similar beliefs.

Palantir expanded its services to the commercial sector, working with businesses in finance, healthcare, and other industries in addition to government contracts. The company's expansion was directed by Karp's strategic vision, which made sure Palantir's technology continued to be applicable and flexible across a broad spectrum of uses. Palantir was able to successfully manage the challenges of growing a technology company thanks to his emphasis on forging close bonds with customers and upholding the highest standards of moral integrity.

Alex Karp

Karp's expertise in philosophy has informed his leadership and innovative attitude throughout this trip. He saw Palantir as a vehicle for bringing about constructive social change as well as a company. Many Palantir employees found resonance in this viewpoint, which helped to create an environment at work that encouraged ethical thought, critical thinking, and a dedication to having a significant influence.

In conclusion, Alex Karp's commitment to ethical technology, entrepreneurial zeal, and philosophical ideas all influenced his journey to starting Palantir Technologies. Karp's path serves as an example of the strength of visionary leadership and the significance of adhering to one's principles in the pursuit of innovation, from his early meetings with Peter Thiel to the difficulties of developing a ground-breaking data analysis platform. His conviction in the ability of technology to handle complicated societal issues while preserving the ideals of privacy and civil rights is reflected in Palantir's success under his direction.

Alex Karp

Getting to know Peter Thiel

An important turning point that led to the establishment of Palantir Technologies was Alex Karp's encounter with Peter Thiel. This was not just a fortuitous meeting; rather, it was a meeting of the minds of people who were interested in philosophy, technology, and its effects on society.

Both Karp and Thiel came from highly scholarly backgrounds; Thiel received his J.D. from Harvard University while Karp received his Ph.D. in philosophy from Stanford University. from the Law School at Stanford. Despite being in separate fields of study, their shared interests provided a foundation for their early relationship. Thiel's interest in the intellectual foundations of innovation and progress aligned with Karp's in-depth philosophical investigations of ethics and societal systems.

Alex Karp

Their meeting conditions stem from Thiel's rise to popularity as a prosperous investor and entrepreneur in the early 2000s. After co-founding PayPal and selling it to eBay for a large profit, Thiel was seeking to fund new projects that shared his belief in using technology to address important issues. He supported initiatives that had the potential to transform entire businesses and, consequently, entire societies, because he was interested in cultivating new ideas.

Conversely, Karp was investigating how to use his philosophical understanding to solve real-world issues. He was especially interested in the moral and practical applications of data to solve difficult problems. It seemed nearly inevitable that Thiel and Karp would cross paths because of their mutual interest in the nexus between technology and societal effect.

Mutual friends in the tech and academic worlds helped bring them together, seeing the potential alignment between Thiel's business savvy and Karp's philosophical outlook. When they eventually got together, it was evident that they had a deep appreciation for the revolutionary potential of technology and data, as well as a dedication to making sure that this potential was used properly.

Karp and Thiel explored the ethical and philosophical aspects of surveillance and data analysis in their talks. They wondered how efficiency and security could be increased through technology without sacrificing civil liberties. These discussions were motivated by a realistic goal to develop instruments that might solve issues in the actual world, not simply theoretical ones.

Thiel was very pleased with Karp's deliberate and morally grounded approach. He perceived in Karp a similar spirit who might offer a distinctive viewpoint on the difficulties facing the tech sector. Thiel shared Karp's emphasis on the ethical consequences of technology and the idea that innovation must be based on solid moral and philosophical ideas.

Alex Karp

Palantir Technologies was founded as a result of this convergence of ideas. They had an idea for a business that would create cutting-edge software for data analysis that could integrate and comprehend enormous volumes of data. The objective was to respect stringent ethical standards to protect civil liberties and privacy while offering organizations meaningful insights.

Thiel was sufficiently convinced by Karp's vision to contribute the initial money for Palantir. This funding, together with Thiel's strategic direction and Karp's inspirational leadership, laid the groundwork for the company's growth. After accepting the position of CEO, Karp oversaw Palantir's expansion and made sure that the company's moral values continued to be central to all aspects of its business dealings.

Karp and Thiel's collaboration turned out to be very successful. Together, Karp's philosophical background and Thiel's economic savvy enabled them to successfully manage the challenges of creating a software company that could ethically handle sensitive data. Their partnership also drew in a group of people who shared their enthusiasm for leveraging technology to improve society.

In conclusion, Alex Karp's encounter with Peter Thiel was a game-changer that brought together their practical and intellectual prowess. The gathering was based on a common understanding of moral innovation and a dedication to using technology to address challenging issues. Palantir Technologies was founded as a result of this collaboration, which also established a benchmark for how IT firms can incorporate philosophical ideas into their business plans. Their partnership continues to influence Palantir's operations and strategy for tackling some of the most important problems of our day.

Palantir Technologies' Inception

An important turning point in the development of data analytics and its application to practical issues was

Alex Karp

marked by the founding of Palantir Technologies. The company's establishment is a result of the vision and tenacity of Joe Lonsdale, Stephen Cohen, Nathan Gettings, Alex Karp, and Peter Thiel. Together, they set out to find a business that would transform the application of data to address some of the most difficult problems that society faces.

Palantir's origins can be found in the early 2000s, when national security concerns were a global concern, especially in the wake of the September 11 attacks. Despite their struggles to meaningfully interpret the massive volumes of data they possessed, governments and organizations were becoming more and more conscious of this fact. To provide actionable intelligence, there was an urgent need for tools that could combine, evaluate, and visualize data from many sources.

After meeting and becoming friends due to their mutual passion for technology and philosophy, Alex Karp and Peter Thiel identified this gap. Thiel contributed a financial and strategic viewpoint due to his experience

Alex Karp

with PayPal and financial knowledge. Karp, on the other hand, established an ethical and philosophical framework, highlighting the necessity of a technology that protected civil liberties and privacy while simultaneously offering sophisticated analytics.

As a result of their conversations, a data analytics platform that could meet these requirements was conceptualized. The goal was quite clear: to create software that would enable enterprises to combine and examine enormous datasets to find previously hidden patterns and insights. Palantir was to be founded on ethical grounds, in contrast to many other digital endeavors. Karp and Thiel insisted that proper usage of their technology should respect people's privacy.

Palantir's early development was characterized by long planning and brainstorming sessions. The co-founders intended for the platform to be easy to use, so analysts with varying degrees of technical proficiency could take advantage of its features. Their goal was to develop software that could be used in a variety of industries, such as banking, healthcare, national security, and more. Obtaining finance was one of the initial difficulties. The original seed money required to launch the initiative was supplied by Thiel's funding. The team needed this financial support to invest in the development of their product and hire top people. As the company's chief executive officer, Karp was instrumental in putting together a group of engineers, data scientists, and analysts who shared the company's moral values and were highly competent.

The process of development was quite demanding. The group had to overcome many technical obstacles to develop a platform that could manage the volume and complexity of data needed. They concentrated on developing a system that could combine data from several sources, guarantee data security, and offer user-friendly visualizations that facilitated result interpretation.

Alex Karp

Securing contracts with government entities was one of Palantir's first significant successes. These initial collaborations were essential in showcasing Palantir's technology's worth. Quick recognition was given to the organization by its capacity to deliver actionable insights from large datasets. Palantir's software, for instance, was crucial in counterterrorism operations, assisting analysts in recognizing and neutralizing such threats.

The creators of Palantir were well aware of the ethical ramifications of their work despite these early triumphs. Karp in particular made a strong case for the necessity of striking a balance between the preservation of individual rights and the advantages of data analytics. The business put strict civil rights and privacy policies into place, making sure that their technology was used in a way that upheld these values. In addition to setting Palantir apart from other digital firms, this moral position promoted stakeholder and customer trust.

Palantir's growth allowed it to go beyond contracts with the government. The business started working with clients in the private sector, utilizing its technology across numerous industries. Palantir's technology has shown to be effective and versatile, serving a range of industries from financial institutions aiming to detect fraud to healthcare organizations looking to enhance patient outcomes.

Palantir Technologies was born not merely as a business but also as a vision come to pass. By effectively creating a platform that revolutionized data analytics, Karp, Thiel, and their co-founders showed how technology might be applied to ethically sound problem-solving techniques. Palantir's expansion and achievements are evidence of their dedication to creativity, morality, and the conviction that data, handled sensibly, can bring about significant global change.

In summary, the history of Palantir Technologies is one of foresight, teamwork, and moral dedication. The company was founded to use data for good, overcoming the difficulties of developing a game-changing technology while upholding civil liberties and privacy laws. Palantir has emerged as a pioneer in the data analytics space under Alex Karp's direction, offering

Alex Karp

solutions that assist businesses in navigating the challenges of the contemporary world.

Academic Contributions and Dissertations

The depth of Alex Karp's intellectual engagement with philosophical issues and their real-world applications is evident in his dissertation and other scholarly works. His doctoral thesis, which examined the moral ramifications of privacy and monitoring, served as the capstone of his academic career and served as the foundation for his subsequent employment at Palantir Technologies.

Karp studied philosophy for his doctorate at Stanford University, where he was mentored by eminent academics in the subject and immersed in rigorous study. His dissertation examined how contemporary surveillance technologies subvert conventional ideas of privacy and civil freedoms. It also focused on the nexus of philosophy, law, and ethics.

The investigation of ethical frameworks that could direct the use of surveillance technology in a way that respects individual rights and social values was at the heart of Karp's dissertation. He examined many philosophical stances and offered substitutes by using ethical ideas to criticize the state of affairs. Karp's approach to work was characterized by its interdisciplinary nature, incorporating ideas from political science, technology, law, and philosophy.

Karp made important scholarly contributions through his books and research in addition to his dissertation. He published in esteemed academic journals, gave talks at conferences and symposiums, and wrote articles addressing difficult philosophical problems about technology and society. His works frequently questioned received wisdom, expanding the purview of philosophy to address modern problems.

Alex Karp

Karp has made significant scholarly contributions, one of which is his support of responsibility and openness in the use of technology. While advances in data analytics and surveillance provide useful instruments for the good of society, he contended that they also present serious ethical problems. Karp promoted moral standards and legal frameworks that could guarantee responsible technology usage while preserving personal liberties.

Furthermore, Karp's scholarly endeavours demonstrated his wider dedication to social justice and human rights. He participated in talks about the moral obligations of technologists and legislators, highlighting the significance of moral introspection and public dialogue. His writings struck a chord with academics and professionals alike, inspiring thoughtful consideration of the consequences of technological progress for democracies.

Karp's academic background helped him mold his viewpoint and equipped him with the skills necessary to take on a leadership position in the technology sector.

Alex Karp

His rigorous philosophical background gave him a strong foundation in critical thinking, ethical reasoning, and a dedication to leading with principles. These attributes would prove crucial in steering Palantir Technologies, where Karp used his philosophical understanding to mold the organization's privacy and data analytics policies.

In conclusion, Alex Karp's dissertation and scholarly works highlight his breadth of knowledge and dedication to using philosophical investigation to confront important societal concerns. His investigation of the morality of technology and monitoring continues to impact discussions in higher education, business, and legislation. Karp's academic background served as a springboard for his business ventures and illustrated the significant influence of philosophical thought on ethical leadership and creativity in the contemporary world.

Alex Karp

First Difficulties and Achievements

Early on, Alex Karp and Palantir Technologies saw several noteworthy setbacks and victories that shaped the company's course and solidified its standing as a pioneer in data analytics.

1. Advancements in Technology:
- Creating a scalable and reliable data analytics platform was a difficult technical task. Palantir had to develop software that could securely, quickly, and accurately combine enormous volumes of disparate data. This necessitated a significant investment in R&D in addition to overcoming technical obstacles in data integration and analysis.

2. Acceptance in the Market:
It was difficult to persuade prospective customers—especially big businesses and government organizations—of the worth and dependability of Palantir's technology. Giving sensitive data to a

relatively young and unknown company made many organizations hesitant. It took thorough platform demonstrations and the building of trust through productive pilot projects to dispel this skepticism.

3. The Regulation and Ethical Aspects:
- Palantir has to negotiate difficult legal environments and moral dilemmas while working in a sensitive industry like data analytics and surveillance. Priorities included ensuring adherence to privacy regulations and resolving issues with data security and individual rights. Palantir's adherence to moral standards and open business practices was essential in reducing these difficulties.

4. Stability of Finances:
- Palantir had financial difficulties in its early years, just like many other businesses. It was crucial to get enough money to maintain continuing operations and investments in technology development. Although Peter Thiel's original donation was a vital lifeline, maintaining

Alex Karp

financial stability necessitated ongoing income stream expansion and strategic planning.

nitial Achievements

1. Strategic Alliances:
- Strategic alliances with clients in the public and private sectors were a major factor in Palantir's early accomplishments. Palantir's technology and skills were validated through the acquisition of contracts from organizations including the Department of Defence and the CIA. Along with bringing in money, these alliances improved Palantir's standing as a reliable source for data analytics products.

2. Uniqueness and Originality:
Palantir set itself apart from rivals by developing proprietary technology and engaging in constant innovation. The business stands out in the industry thanks to its capacity to manage challenging data integration issues and deliver useful insights. Palantir's innovations, including Gotham, which was created for

intelligence and law enforcement organizations, demonstrated the company's technological capabilities and capacity to cater to specific requirements.

3. Entering New Markets:
- Building on its early success in securing government contracts, Palantir expanded into other industries like energy, healthcare, and finance to broaden its clientele. Palantir's platform's versatility enabled it to tackle a wide range of industry-specific issues, such as detecting fraud in financial transactions and improving patient care in hospital environments. Palantir's revenue streams and market reach were expanded by this development.

4. Influence and Thought Leadership:
Palantir made a name for itself as a thought leader in data analytics and tech ethics, going beyond financial measurements. Palantir's reputation was improved by Alex Karp's support of responsible data use and his participation in public discussions on the societal effects of technology. The organization's enduring prosperity may be attributed to its dedication to ethical governance,

Alex Karp

transparency, and safeguarding civil freedoms, which struck a chord with stakeholders.

Through creativity, strategic alliances, and a dedication to moral values, Alex Karp and Palantir Technologies overcame early difficulties. Palantir's development and leadership in the data analytics sector can be attributed to its early triumphs. Palantir showed tenacity and vision by taking on technological, legal, and commercial obstacles head-on, becoming a leader in the use of data for social good while respecting moral principles.

Alex Karp

CHAPTER 3: LEADERSHIP AND PHILOSOPHY IN BUSINESS

Palantir Technologies' leadership under Alex Karp is distinguished by a special fusion of strategic vision, ethical issues, and philosophical clarity. His business philosophy is based on a strong dedication to using technology to advance society while maintaining the values of openness, responsibility, and respect for human liberties.

Foundational Philosophy

Karp's Ph.D. from Stanford University and philosophy background have a big impact on his leadership style and strategic choices at Palantir. Karp views philosophy as a useful instrument for ethical thinking and decision-making in the corporate world, not only an

Alex Karp

academic endeavor. He highlights the significance of posing fundamental queries regarding the effects of technology on society, the moral ramifications of data use, and the obligations of digital firms to protect civil rights and privacy.

Moral Guidance

Karp's leadership philosophy is based on a strong commitment to moral principles. According to him, technology should be created and applied in ways that maximize good and minimize harm to society. Karp has led efforts at Palantir to incorporate morality into the company's operations and culture. This entails putting in place strong privacy safeguards, abiding by best practices for data security, and supporting laws that encourage accountability and openness.

Beyond simply following the rules, Karp aspires to establish industry norms for responsible data usage and governance. This is an example of his ethical leadership. His openness regarding Palantir's processes and his

Alex Karp

advocacy for transparency in technological operations are intended to foster confidence among stakeholders, including the public, employees, and clients. In addition to improving Palantir's reputation, this open approach encourages an ethical and morally responsible culture within the organization.

Strategic Perspective

In his capacity as CEO, Karp has been instrumental in determining Palantir's growth and strategic orientation. He has managed the creation of cutting-edge data analytics platforms serving a variety of sectors, including healthcare, energy, and government as well as finance. In a software industry that is changing quickly, Karp's strategic vision highlights the value of flexibility and agility to keep Palantir at the forefront of technical innovation.

Palantir has broadened its clientele and increased its global reach under Karp's direction, showcasing the technology's adaptability to a variety of industries. His strategy choices are informed by a long-term view of how Palantir's products will affect society, to generate long-term value for clients while advancing objectives like increasing security, boosting efficiency, and encouraging moral data practices.

Organizational Culture and Staff Engagement

Karp is a big believer in creating a welcoming and cooperative workplace atmosphere at Palantir. He is a proponent of giving staff members the freedom to innovate, think critically, and support the goals of the business. Within the company, Karp fosters candid discussion and communication, fostering a cooperative atmosphere that values a range of viewpoints.

His style of leadership places a strong emphasis on professional development and mentoring, making sure that staff members have the chance to advance and prosper at Palantir. Top talent in tech and analytics seek out Palantir as an attractive employer, partly due to

Alex Karp

Karp's dedication to developing talent and cultivating a culture of constant learning.

Public Participation and Thought Leadership

In addition to his position at Palantir, Alex Karp is regarded as a leading authority on matters pertaining to the convergence of technology, ethics, and society. He participates in panels, gives speeches at conferences, and writes articles that question the status quo and promote responsible IT usage. He is an active participant in public discourse. Karp is a thought leader who influences industry standards and regulatory frameworks by promoting policies that strike a balance between innovation and ethical issues.

Palantir Technologies' leadership under Alex Karp is a prime example of a comprehensive strategy that incorporates ethical standards, strategic vision, philosophical contemplation, and a dedication to social impact. His emphasis on openness, moral leadership, and responsible innovation has established a standard for

Alex Karp

how digital firms can handle morally challenging situations while fostering innovation and expansion. Palantir's course and the broader tech industry's attitude to ethical tech development and deployment are both shaped by Karp's visionary leadership.

The CEO of Philosopher

It is common to refer to Alex Karp as the "Philosopher CEO," a moniker that honors his distinct philosophical background and the significant impact it has had on his leadership approach, strategic choices, and moral judgments at Palantir Technologies.

Philosophical Background

Karp's scholastic endeavors laid the foundation for his career as a Philosopher CEO. After receiving his Ph.D. in philosophy from Stanford University, he studied political philosophy, ethical theories, and the social effects of technology. He possessed a comprehensive perspective on difficult ethical conundrums, analytical rigor, and critical thinking abilities thanks to his philosophical background. In addition to molding Karp's perspective, this academic background offered a structure for handling ethical and social problems in the corporate sector.

Moral Guidance and Principles

Karp's philosophy is centered on the importance of values-driven decision-making and ethical leadership. According to him, technology should be created and used properly, keeping in mind how it could affect both people and society as a whole. Palantir's commercial operations have been guided by Karp's advocacy of transparency, accountability, and respect for privacy rights in the use of data analytics.

Alex Karp

To secure sensitive data, Palantir has put in place strict data security and privacy procedures under Karp's direction. He highlights the significance of moral governance systems that put stakeholders' interests first while encouraging growth and innovation. In addition to influencing Palantir's corporate culture, Karp's moral leadership has established the business as a pioneer in ethical data analytics and technological solutions.

Philosophy and Business Strategy Integration

In his capacity as CEO, Karp has infused philosophical ideas into Palantir's operations and business plan. He pushes staff members to make deliberate decisions and use ethical thinking. Karp's focus on the moral consequences of technological progress has sparked conversations about the wider societal effects of Palantir's work among Palantir employees.

Palantir's strategic efforts are guided by philosophy, which affects how the business handles difficult problems including product development, client

Alex Karp

relationships, and regulatory compliance. Palantir can adapt to shifting social norms and ethical standards because of Karp's philosophy, which promotes ongoing introspection and evaluation.

Public Advocacy and Thought Leadership

In addition to his position at Palantir, thought leader and proponent of moral tech practices Alex Karp is well-known. He speaks about data privacy, the ethical implications of technology, and the role of companies in creating a responsible digital ecosystem at conferences, public forums, and interviews. Karp's public advocacy involves influencing industry norms and policy discussions, as well as advocating for moral standards that strike a balance between innovation and social issues.

Effect on Innovation and Culture at Palantir

Alex Karp

The innovation spirit and corporate culture of Palantir have been greatly influenced by Karp's ideas. He cultivates an environment at work where integrity, ethical integrity, and intellectual curiosity are valued. Karp pushes staff members to question presumptions, exercise critical thought, and support Palantir's goal of applying data analytics to improve society.

Under his direction, Palantir has persisted in innovating and growing its capabilities in a variety of industries, including energy, finance, healthcare, and government. For businesses looking for cutting-edge data analytics solutions, Palantir is known as a reliable partner thanks to Karp's innovative leadership and dedication to moral values.

The incorporation of philosophical thought into business leadership is best demonstrated by Alex Karp in his capacity as the Philosopher CEO. His philosophical upbringing has influenced his support for ethical tech practices at Palantir Technologies, as well as his ethical leadership style and strategic decision-making. Karp's dedication to moral rectitude, openness, and social impact establishes a standard for how Internet firms can handle difficult moral dilemmas while fostering innovation and long-term expansion. In his role as CEO of Philosopher, Alex Karp continues to shape the way the tech sector approaches ethical tech development and governance, encouraging a responsible innovation culture and social responsibility.

The Leadership Style of Karp

Palantir Technologies's Alex Karp is a leader who combines strategic brilliance, philosophical depth, and a strong sense of ethical integrity. His management style has been crucial in forming Palantir's corporate culture, spurring creativity, and negotiating the intricacies of the IT sector.

Enlightened Guidance

Alex Karp

Palantir Technologies has a compelling and distinct vision that serves as the foundation for Karp's leadership. He describes a time in the future when ethical standards and individual rights will be respected and data analytics will be used to benefit society. This forward-thinking perspective motivates stakeholders and staff alike, giving the company a feeling of direction and purpose.

Making Strategic Decisions

In his role as CEO, Karp exhibits a sharp ability to make judgment calls that set Palantir up for long-term success. He places a strong emphasis on flexibility and agility since he understands how quickly technology is advancing and how this affects corporate strategy. Karp frequently makes strategic decisions that are informed by his in-depth knowledge of client demands, market dynamics, and new developments in technology and data analytics.

Integrity in Ethics

Alex Karp

Integrity in ethics is a core component of Karp's leadership style. In all facets of Palantir's business operations, he promotes responsibility, openness, and responsible data use. Beyond merely adhering to regulations, Karp's ethical position takes into account civil freedoms, privacy rights, and the overall effects of technology on society. Palantir is known as a reliable partner and a pioneer in ethical tech practices thanks to his emphasis on ethical governance.

Innovative Thinking and Leadership

In the tech sector, Karp is regarded as a thought leader. He frequently participates in public discussions on topics like artificial intelligence, data privacy, and the moral implications of technology. His advocacy for industrial norms that give ethical considerations priority and his ability to influence policy debates are examples of his thought leadership. At Palantir, Karp fosters an innovative culture that gives staff members the freedom to experiment, question conventional wisdom, and push the limits of data analytics skills.

Teamwork and Diversity

At Palantir, Karp promotes an inclusive and cooperative leadership approach. He cherishes different viewpoints and promotes candid discussion within the company. Karp encourages a culture in which workers are encouraged to express their opinions and concerns, which fosters a vibrant and innovative workplace. His style of leadership places a strong emphasis on respect for one another, cooperation, and the group's pursuit of organizational objectives.

Adaptable and Resilient

As Karp leads Palantir through opportunities and challenges, he demonstrates flexibility and resilience. He exhibits flexibility in reaction to shifting market conditions and technology breakthroughs while staying unwavering in his dedication to Palantir's purpose and

Alex Karp

ideals. Karp's capacity for strategic change and long-term thinking has been essential to Palantir's development into one of the industry's top suppliers of data analytics solutions.

Development and Mentoring

At Palantir, Karp places a lot of focus on professional growth and mentoring. He thinks it's important to develop future leaders, nurture talent, and promote a culture of lifelong learning. Beyond technical expertise, Karp provides mentoring in the areas of ethical reasoning, leadership, and personal development. His commitment to staff development helps Palantir draw and hold on to the best personnel in the cutthroat IT sector.

At Palantir Technologies, Alex Karp's leadership style combines inclusive leadership techniques, strategic decision-making, ethical integrity, and visionary thinking. His philosophical training shapes Palantir's

Alex Karp

culture and strategic direction, influencing his approach to ethical governance and societal effect. Palantir has benefited greatly from Karp's leadership in establishing the company as a pioneer in data analytics innovation while maintaining the values of openness, responsibility, and respect for individual rights. In his role as CEO, Alex Karp continues to provide an example of moral leadership in the tech sector by inspiring and guiding Palantir toward its goal of using data for positive societal effects.

Organizational Culture

At Palantir Technologies, Alex Karp has built a unique corporate culture that is a reflection of his ethical principles, strategic outlook, and philosophical background. Palantir's culture is distinguished by its focus on innovation, honesty, teamwork, and a

Alex Karp

dedication to using responsible data analytics to have a beneficial social impact.

Moral Basis

Strong ethical principles that are supported by Alex Karp are fundamental to Palantir's corporate culture. Karp has made ethical issues a top priority in every facet of Palantir's business from the company's founding. This entails strict adherence to data security procedures, privacy laws, and open business practices that maintain the confidence of stakeholders, partners, and clients. The company's ethical framework aims to set the benchmark for responsible data use and governance in the industry, rather than just complying with rules.

Creativity and Intellectual Interest

Employee creativity and intellectual curiosity are fostered by Palantir's culture. Karp is a firm believer in giving teams the freedom to experiment, question

Alex Karp

conventional wisdom, and push the limits of data analytics. R&D investments, where teams are encouraged to experiment with cutting-edge technology and approaches to address challenging challenges for clients across diverse sectors, promote this innovative culture.

Cooperation and Unity

Palantir bases its approach to problem-solving on collaboration. Karp stresses the value of open communication, respect for one another, and teamwork inside the company. Cross-functional cooperation is promoted to take advantage of different viewpoints and areas of competence, guaranteeing holistic solutions that successfully satisfy client needs. Employee solidarity and collective accountability are fostered by Palantir's collaborative culture, which promotes shared objectives and group accomplishments.

Mentoring and Leadership Development

Alex Karp

At Palantir, Alex Karp is a big believer in mentoring and leadership development. He thinks that developing talent and giving future organization leaders more authority is important. Beyond technical expertise, Karp offers mentoring in ethical reasoning, strategic thinking, and personal development. Palantir creates a pool of competent workers who are prepared to lead innovation and uphold the company's principles by funding leadership development initiatives and career advancement chances.

Inclusion and Diversity

Diversity and inclusivity are important aspects of Palantir's corporate culture. Karp understands the value of a variety of viewpoints in promoting creativity and innovation. The organization values diversity and encourages people with varied experiences, backgrounds, and points of view to feel free to share their special perspectives. Palantir is dedicated to promoting diversity in the workplace and IT sector

Alex Karp

through outreach programs, employee engagement campaigns, and recruiting procedures.

Impact and Attention to the Customer

Palantir's culture is firmly anchored in its dedication to improving society and its customer-centric philosophy. Karp pushes staff members to put clients' interests first and provide solutions that successfully handle problems encountered in the real world. In addition to financial indicators, the company's success is evaluated based on its capacity to add value for customers, boost security, optimize operations, and promote social objectives including public safety, medical progress, and other areas.

Accountability and Transparency

Palantir's relationships with stakeholders are governed by two fundamental principles: accountability and transparency. Karp is a firm believer in keeping lines of communication open and giving information on

Alex Karp

company policies, procedures, and decision-making procedures. Strong bonds and trust are established with clients, partners, regulators, and the community at large as a result of this transparency. Palantir sets an example for ethical business practices in the tech sector by holding itself to high standards of corporate governance, regulatory compliance, and ethical conduct.

Palantir Technologies is currently renowned for its inventive spirit, moral rectitude, and dedication to societal impact thanks to Alex Karp's leadership. Karp's philosophical beliefs are reflected in Palantir's corporate culture, which places a strong emphasis on diversity, ethics, creativity, teamwork, and customer attention. Under his leadership, Palantir has created an environment at work where people are motivated to innovate, work together, and make a significant contribution to the company's goal of applying data analytics to address some of the most important problems facing the globe.

Alex Karp

Palantir's values and ethics

Every facet of Palantir Technologies' operations is guided by a strong ethical framework and core values, which have been established by Alex Karp. Palantir's identity is based on these ethics and values, which also shape the company's approach to technological development, client relations, and societal effects.

Dedication to Data Security and Privacy

Palantir's unwavering dedication to data security and privacy is the first step toward ethical honesty. Acknowledging the delicate nature of the data the organization handles, Karp has put strict procedures in place to preserve private data and individual rights. To assure compliance with international privacy legislation and to reduce the risks associated with data breaches or misuse, Palantir's technology is constructed with integrated privacy features and data anonymization capabilities.

Accountability and Transparency

One of the pillars of Palantir's moral behavior is transparency. Karp stresses the value of being transparent and communicative in all dealings with stakeholders, partners, employees, and clients. The organization endeavors to cultivate trust and confidence among its stakeholders by offering lucid explanations of its technologies, methodology, and decision-making processes. Palantir frequently audits its processes and policies to guarantee compliance with ethical principles and legal obligations. Palantir holds itself accountable to high standards of ethical conduct and corporate governance.

Appropriate Technology Use

Alex Karp

Palantir is dedicated to using technology responsibly to advance society. According to Karp and his group, technology should be used to improve security, increase efficiency, and find solutions to complicated issues that affect corporations, governments, and other institutions. Palantir is committed to promoting social justice, safeguarding human rights, and upholding civil liberties through the responsible and ethical use of its technologies. To this end, the company is focused on creating best practices and ethical principles for data analytics.

Preserving Civil Liberties and Human Rights

Alex Karp is an advocate for civil liberties and human rights preservation in the application of Palantir's technologies. He actively advocates for the creation of ethical frameworks that give human rights issues priority since he understands the potential impact that data analytics can have on both persons and communities. Palantir collaborates closely with advocacy groups, human rights organizations, and other relevant parties to address moral dilemmas and reduce the risks that come with making decisions based mostly on statistics.

Inclusion, Equity, and Diversity

Diversity, equity, and inclusion are important aspects of Palantir's ethical culture. Karp is a firm believer in fostering an environment at work where people with different experiences, backgrounds, and viewpoints are recognized, valued, and given the freedom to share their special ideas. To create a workforce that reflects the diverse communities it serves around the world, the corporation supports diversity in hiring policies, employee development programs, and leadership opportunities.

Corporate Responsibility and Its Effect on Society

Palantir is committed to using its technology and business operations to positively benefit society, and this commitment is driven by ethical ideals. Karp urges staff members to prioritize projects that support Palantir's

Alex Karp

objective of leveraging data analytics to address global concerns and to think about the broader ramifications of their work. The business works with governmental bodies, charitable groups, and educational establishments to address topics including environmental sustainability, public health, and disaster response, among others.

Ethical Advocacy and Leadership

Alex Karp leverages his position as a thought leader in the tech sector to promote moral leadership and conscientious use of technology. He takes part in policy discussions, holds public forums, and advocates for industry-wide projects that raise the bar for moral behavior in data analytics and technological innovation. Karp's lobbying efforts encompass molding public understanding of ethical problems in the digital age as well as influencing regulatory frameworks.
Alex Karp's commitment to ethical integrity, responsible innovation, and societal impact is demonstrated by his ethics and principles at Palantir Technologies. Karp has

fostered a culture of ethical excellence at Palantir by placing a high value on privacy, transparency, responsible technology use, human rights, diversity, and corporate responsibility. The company has continued to set industry norms for moral behavior under his direction, proving that moral leadership and financial success are compatible in the tech sector.

Handling Differing Opinions

Leaders in prominent roles must always navigate controversy, and Palantir Technologies CEO Alex Karp has had his fair share of controversy over the years. His treatment of these matters demonstrates his strategic thinking, dedication to openness, and moral values.

Honesty and Direct Communication

Open communication and transparency are essential components of Karp's approach to handling conflicts. Karp has placed a high value on open and honest

Alex Karp

communication whenever Palantir has been embroiled in a controversy, be it with government contracts, data privacy issues, or the moral implications of its technology. This strategy seeks to directly address the concerns of stakeholders, contextualize difficult problems, and show responsibility for the company's actions.

Interacting with Interest Groups

Karp is a proponent of taking a proactive approach when handling disputes involving clients, staff members, investors, authorities, and the general public. Palantir aims to preserve positive connections and regain people's trust by paying attention to issues, owning up to mistakes, and committing to corrective steps when needed. Palantir strives to learn from controversies and improve its practices and policies, and Karp's leadership makes sure that the company accepts accountability for its actions.

Preserving Moral Principles

Alex Karp

Karp highlights Palantir's dedication to sustaining moral principles and conscientious business practices when handling disputes. To guarantee that Palantir's actions are consistent with its values of privacy, data security, and respect for human rights, he promotes moral decision-making at all organizational levels. Palantir wants to show its commitment to ethical governance and reduce the risks that come with controversies by upholding a strong ethical framework.

Education and Adjustment

Disputes frequently present chances for growth and adjustment. At Palantir, Karp promotes a culture of continuous improvement whereby lessons from controversies are applied to fortify regulations, improve transparency protocols, and hone operational procedures. Palantir reveals its commitment to constructively addressing concerns and adjusting to changing expectations by welcoming feedback and being open to change.

Alex Karp

Upholding Conviction-Based Principles

Karp has demonstrated a willingness to stand up for Palantir's values and technological advancements in the face of controversy. He explains the company's stance on divisive topics, dispels myths, and emphasizes how Palantir's technology helps solve pressing problems for businesses, governments, and society as a whole. Karp's unwavering commitment to Palantir's mission and values boosts the company's standing in the face of controversy and fosters trust among stakeholders.

Sector Guidance and Promotion

In addition to handling internal conflicts, Karp advocates for more extensive industry reforms and moral guidelines. He engages in public discussions, participates in policy debates, and collaborates with industry peers to promote responsible tech practices and regulatory frameworks. By advocating for transparency, accountability, and ethical governance across the tech sector, Karp aims to shape industry norms and enhance public trust in technology companies.

Alex Karp's approach to navigating controversies at Palantir Technologies reflects his strategic leadership, commitment to transparency, and ethical integrity. By prioritizing open communication, engaging with stakeholders, upholding ethical standards, and advocating for industry reforms, Karp aims to address controversies constructively and strengthen Palantir's reputation as a responsible leader in the tech industry. His leadership underscores the importance of ethical governance and principled decision-making in maintaining trust and driving long-term success in a rapidly evolving technological landscape.

Handling Public and Political Scrutiny

Alex Karp, as CEO of Palantir Technologies, has weathered several situations of public and political criticism throughout his tenure. His approach to tackling these difficulties demonstrates strategic vision, ethical considerations, and a commitment to transparent communication.

Strategic Response to Public Scrutiny

When faced with public scrutiny, particularly about Palantir's technology and its uses, Karp emphasizes a strategic approach anchored in transparency and clarity. He realizes the necessity of addressing issues directly, offering factual information about Palantir's goods and services, and dispelling misconceptions that may occur in public conversation. By proactively engaging with the public through interviews, conferences, and media releases, Karp wants to build the narrative surrounding Palantir and its contributions to many industries.

Ethical Considerations and Accountability

Ethical issues are fundamental in Karp's approach to facing public and political scrutiny. He stresses Palantir's commitment to ethical governance, data protection, and human rights in all interactions with stakeholders. When disputes arise, Karp highlights the company's adherence to ethical principles and its efforts to promote transparency and accountability in its operations. This pledge helps minimize concerns and reinforces Palantir's reputation as a good corporate citizen.

Engaging with Political Stakeholders

Given Palantir's considerable participation with government agencies and public sector clients, Karp navigates political scrutiny by developing positive connections with political influencers. He understands the necessity of understanding regulatory frameworks, complying with legal requirements, and cooperating with legislators to address concerns connected to data security, privacy, and the ethical implications of technology use. By interacting proactively with political players, Karp tries to create trust, influence policy conversations, and contribute to the development of acceptable regulatory frameworks.

Alex Karp

Upholding Technological Advancements

When Palantir's technological inventions come under public and political scrutiny, Karp argues that they have a positive impact on society and defend the company's innovations. He draws attention to how Palantir's data analytics platforms may revolutionize the way that governments and companies make crucial decisions by boosting security, increasing efficiency, and enabling these processes. Karp seeks to dispel misunderstandings and address worries about Palantir's technology while showcasing real-world applications and success stories.

Open Communication

Karp bases his strategy for dealing with political and public scrutiny on transparency. He thinks that stakeholders should be given thorough and understandable information about Palantir's rules, procedures, and activities. This entails being transparent about difficulties, owning up to errors, and detailing the company's corrective measures. Open communication

Alex Karp

promotes accountability, increases trust, and allows for fruitful discussion with the public, political figures, and regulatory bodies.

Education and Adjustment

Karp sees occasions of political and public scrutiny as chances for growth and adjustment. He exhorts Palantir to consider stakeholder concerns while implementing changes, reviewing its procedures, and incorporating input. Karp makes sure Palantir adapts to changing demands in the IT business and is robust in the face of criticism by fostering a culture of responsiveness and constant improvement.

Sector Guidance and Promotion

Beyond handling issues within the company, Karp advocates for ethical standards and industry-wide reforms through his leadership role. To advance ethical tech practices and openness in regulations, he takes part in industry forums, advocates for the public, and works

Alex Karp

with peers. Karp hopes to increase Palantir's standing as a pioneer in ethical digital innovation, impact industry standards, and drive policy discussions by promoting ethical governance and accountability throughout the tech sector.

Alex Karp demonstrates his strategic leadership, ethical integrity, and commitment to open communication in the way he handles political and public scrutiny at Palantir Technologies. Through a focus on ethical concerns, strategic response, stakeholder involvement, and advocacy for technological advancements, Karp adeptly navigates challenging situations and upholds Palantir's reputation as a reliable and responsible partner in the tech industry. His leadership demonstrates how crucial moral leadership and moral judgment are to controlling political and public criticism, promoting sustainable growth, and having an impact on society.

Alex Karp

CHAPTER 4: GROWTH AND EXPANSION

During his time as CEO of Palantir Technologies, Alex Karp has overseen major development and expansion projects. The company has improved its global position in the competitive data analytics and technology solutions market, expanded its capabilities, and diversified its clientele under its direction.

A Strategic Growth Vision

Karp's strategic plan for Palantir's expansion focuses on using data analytics to tackle the difficult problems that businesses, governments, and other organizations confront globally. He highlights how Palantir's platforms can revolutionize a variety of industries by boosting operational effectiveness, facilitating better decision-making, and stimulating creativity. Palantir's strategic efforts are guided by Karp's forward-thinking approach, which ensures alignment with developing trends in data science and technology as well as market prospects.

Service Diversification

Palantir has expanded its services beyond its initial emphasis on government contracts under Karp's direction. The business now offers data analytics solutions designed specifically for sectors like manufacturing, healthcare, finance, and energy. Palantir's diversification approach allows it to increase its global market reach and cater to a wide range of client needs. Palantir is enhancing its value portfolio and solidifying its position as a reliable partner for businesses looking for cutting-edge data-driven insights by creating specialized platforms and applications.

International Growth and Market Infiltration

Alex Karp

Under Karp's direction, Palantir has conducted vigorous worldwide expansion initiatives, creating a presence in important markets throughout North America, Europe, Asia-Pacific, and beyond. The company's expansion strategy entails setting up additional offices, developing strategic alliances with nearby companies and governmental organizations, and modifying its technological platforms to satisfy local legal needs and consumer requests. Palantir's capacity to service multinational clients and take advantage of new opportunities in the global marketplace is improved by its worldwide footprint.

Technological Innovation and Progress

Karp sees innovation as a key driver of Palantir's expansion. To expand its skills in data analytics, improve platform features, and incorporate cutting-edge technologies like machine learning and artificial intelligence, the company makes significant investments in research and development. Palantir's dedication to technology innovation helps them to keep one step ahead of rivals and provide creative solutions that tackle changing customer demands and business obstacles.

Strategic Alliances and Cooperatives

Under Karp's direction, Palantir's growth strategy heavily relies on strategic alliances. To spur innovation, jointly develop solutions, and break into new markets, the company works with top technological companies, academic institutions, and industry professionals. Through these collaborations, Palantir's ecosystem of stakeholders is strengthened, industry best practices are promoted, and knowledge is is is exchanged. Palantir strengthens its competitive edge and broadens its sphere of influence in the international IT community by forming strategic relationships.

Expanding Organizational Development and Operations

Under Karp's direction, Palantir has scaled its operations and made investments in organizational development programs to support its growth trajectory. To strengthen its staff and skills, the company hires elite talent in a variety of fields, including data science, engineering, sales, and customer service. Palantir prioritizes internal innovation and talent development by fostering a culture of continuous learning, employee training, and career growth. In the fast-paced tech sector, Palantir prepares itself for long-term growth and scalability by improving worker agility and operational efficiency.

Market positioning and strategic acquisitions

Palantir has targeted strategic acquisitions in addition to organic expansion to broaden its market reach, hire people, and improve its technological portfolio. Karp is in charge of assessing and incorporating acquisition candidates that support Palantir's strategic goals and quickening the company's expansion. Palantir can expand its product line, penetrate new market niches, and improve its competitiveness in the international market thanks to these acquisitions.

Alex Karp

Palantir Technologies' development and expansion as a top supplier of technological solutions and data analytics has been made possible in large part by Alex Karp's leadership. His innovative approach, emphasis on growth internationally, strategic alliances, organizational development programs, and calculated acquisitions have set Palantir up for long-term success in a cutthroat market that is changing quickly. Under Karp's direction, Palantir keeps innovating, growing in the market, and providing significant solutions that enable businesses to use data to achieve game-changing results.

The Rise of Palantir

Under Alex Karp's direction, Palantir Technologies has made a spectacular ascent from its inception to emerge as a major force in the data analytics and technology solutions sector. The ascent can be ascribed to multiple pivotal elements that have molded Palantir's development and prosperity.

Alex Karp

Origins and Formative Years

A group of former PayPal employees, including Peter Thiel, Alex Karp, Joe Lonsdale, Stephen Cohen, and Nathan Gettings, created Palantir Technologies in 2003. To support government agencies in their counterterrorism operations, the company's original goal was to develop software that could combine, organize, and analyze huge volumes of data. Palantir's future expansion and specialization in data analytics were made possible by this fundamental focus on data integration and analysis.

Strategic Alliances and Government Contracts

Early on, Palantir was able to land big contracts with the government, mostly in the intelligence and defense ministries. Differentiating itself from competitors, the company was able to create specialized software systems that could manage classified and sensitive data. Palantir's technology supported national security and law enforcement initiatives with its sophisticated skills in data fusion, pattern recognition, and predictive analytics.

Growth Into Business Sectors

Palantir extended its services into commercial markets, such as finance, healthcare, energy, and manufacturing, building on its success in the public sector. The business modified its data analytics systems to handle problems unique to certain industries, including supply chain optimization in manufacturing, patient care optimization in healthcare, fraud detection in financial transactions, and operational efficiency improvements in the energy sector.

Innovation and Advancements in Technology

Technology innovation has been Palantir's top priority as a growth engine under Alex Karp's direction. To improve the scalability and performance of its platforms, incorporate cutting-edge technologies like artificial intelligence and machine learning, and strengthen its

Alex Karp

data analytics capabilities, the company makes significant investments in research and development. Palantir's ability to stay ahead of the competition and provide innovative solutions that satisfy changing customer needs is a result of its ongoing innovation.

Market penetration and worldwide reach

Under Karp's direction, Palantir has increased its presence throughout the world by opening offices in important cities in North America, Europe, Asia-Pacific, and other areas. To increase its market presence and meet local market demands, the company has forged strategic alliances with national and international organizations as well as local enterprises. Palantir is positioned as a global leader in data analytics solutions because of its ability to service multinational clients and enter a variety of industrial verticals.

Cultural Focus on Responsibilities and Ethics

Alex Karp

Palantir has consistently placed a high value on morality, accountability, and openness in its business practices. Under Alex Karp's direction, Palantir's technology has been implemented with a focus on civil liberties, data privacy protection, and moral governance. Palantir's dedication to moral values has made it a dependable partner for stakeholders and clients, which has increased its legitimacy and sustainability in the cutthroat tech sector.

Adjusting to the Dynamics and Obstacles of the Market

Palantir's success has been largely attributed to its capacity to adjust to shifting market conditions and deal with business obstacles. To improve its offerings, hone its strategy, and keep a competitive advantage, the company keeps a close eye on legislative changes, client feedback, and market trends. Palantir can efficiently traverse hurdles and grasp growth possibilities due to its agility and responsiveness to market needs. This helps the company maintain its success in a competitive and dynamic business climate.

Alex Karp

Under Alex Karp's direction, Palantir Technologies has grown from a government-focused company to a worldwide renowned leader in data analytics and technological solutions. Palantir has established itself as a reliable partner for businesses looking for cutting-edge data-driven insights and solutions through smart government contracts, forays into commercial markets, technological innovation, global reach, ethical governance, and adaptable tactics. Palantir continues to develop, grow its market share, and have a positive impact on a variety of industries under Karp's direction, establishing a standard for moral leadership and technological innovation in the digital era.

Growth into Novel Markets

Palantir Technologies has strategically entered new markets under Alex Karp's direction, broadening its clientele and reaching beyond its original areas of concentration. Growing Palantir's influence and revenue streams in several industries has been made possible in large part by this development.

Finding Market Possibilities

Palantir's strategy for entering new sectors starts with spotting good prospects where its data analytics know-how can solve big problems and create value. Karp and his group carry out in-depth market research to comprehend industry-specific requirements, new trends, and possible customer pain points. Palantir can give priority to industries that are ready for innovation and where its technology may have a significant impact because of this proactive strategy.

Tailoring Solutions to Industry Requirements

Every industry has different needs and challenges, thus Palantir must provide solutions specifically designed to meet those needs. Karp emphasizes how Palantir's platforms can be tailored to fit the unique needs of various industries, including manufacturing, energy,

Alex Karp

healthcare, finance, and more. Palantir's technologies, for instance, are tailored for risk management, fraud detection, and compliance monitoring in the banking industry patient care optimization,, and medical research support in the healthcare industry.

Collaborating with Sector Pioneers

Palantir works with leaders and experts in the business to improve its comprehension of possibilities and problems unique to the sector. These collaborations make it easier to share knowledge, co-develop solutions, and gain access to domain expertise, all of which help Palantir become more relevant and credible in new markets. Palantir creates strategic partnerships to promote its expansion ambitions by lining up with important stakeholders, such as governmental organizations, international enterprises, and academic institutions.

Regional Growth

Alex Karp

Under Karp's direction, Palantir's growth plan also heavily relies on geographic development. In important international markets including North America, Europe, Asia-Pacific, and the Middle East, the corporation opens regional offices and expands its activities. Palantir's physical presence enables the company to better service local customers, adjust to local regulatory frameworks, and seize regionally specific market possibilities. Palantir improves its market penetration and fortifies its ties with local stakeholders by carefully growing its footprint.

Adjusting to Rules and Regulations

Compliance with a variety of regulatory frameworks and data protection legislation is frequently necessary when entering new markets. Palantir prioritizes successfully managing regulatory obstacles, making sure that its products respect regional laws while upholding the highest standards of data security and privacy. Through his leadership, Karp makes sure Palantir keeps up with regulatory changes and modifies its operations

Alex Karp

accordingly, building confidence and trust with both regulatory bodies and clients.

Expanding Functional Abilities

Palantir scales its operational capabilities to fulfill increasing customer needs and support long-term business growth as it enters new markets. This entails bringing in top talent from a variety of fields, improving the infrastructure and support systems, and funding training initiatives to provide staff members with knowledge unique to their industries. Palantir prepares itself for long-term success and scalability in a variety of market settings by creating scalable operational frameworks.

Originality and Distinction

Palantir needs to stand out from the competition when it enters new markets. Karp encourages teams to create innovative solutions and use cutting-edge technology like machine learning and artificial intelligence in its platforms to cultivate an innovative culture within the organization. By consistently pushing the limits of data analytics capabilities, Palantir sets itself apart from rivals and maintains its position as an industry leader in technology-driven solutions.

Palantir Technologies' successful entry into new markets has been largely attributed to Alex Karp's leadership, which has allowed the company to use its knowledge of data analytics to solve a variety of business issues and seize development prospects. Palantir is expanding its global reach through a range of strategies, including strategic market identification, solution customization, industry collaborations, regional expansion, regulatory compliance, operational scalability, and ongoing innovation. Palantir is positioned as a reliable partner for businesses looking for cutting-edge data-driven insights and game-changing solutions in a world that is becoming more digital and networked thanks to Karp's strategic vision and unwavering dedication to excellence.

Alex Karp

Innovations in Technology

Palantir Technologies, led by Alex Karp, has been at the forefront of technological innovation in software development and data analytics. Palantir has developed innovative solutions to solve difficult problems in a variety of industries thanks to Karp's strategic vision and dedication to pushing the frontiers of technology.

Fundamental Technologies

A key component of Palantir's technological advancements is the creation of fundamental platforms that facilitate complex data integration, analysis, and visualization. Palantir Foundry and Palantir Gotham, two of the company's software platforms, are effective instruments that help enterprises handle vast amounts of heterogeneous data, find relevant insights, and come to well-informed decisions. These systems are made to use cutting-edge analytics and algorithms to manage a variety of data sources, including unstructured text, multimedia, and structured databases.

Fusion and Integration of Data

Palantir's capacity for data fusion and integration is one of its primary technological advancements. The business is excellent at gathering data from various sources—regardless of format or location—and combining it into a cohesive ecosystem. With the aid of this skill, businesses can dismantle data silos, obtain comprehensive perspectives on intricate datasets, and obtain in-depth knowledge that informs strategic decision-making. Palantir's proficiency in data fusion amplifies situational awareness, boosts operational efficiency, and facilitates real-time analysis across a variety of applications.

Machine Learning and Advanced Analytics

Alex Karp

Palantir enhances data processing and predictive modeling by incorporating machine learning and advanced analytics into its platforms. Automated data analysis, anomaly identification, pattern recognition, and the creation of predictive insights are made possible by these technologies. Palantir helps companies in a variety of industries, from supply chain management and cybersecurity to finance and healthcare, identify hidden patterns, predict trends, and improve operational procedures. It does this by utilizing machine learning algorithms.

Collaboration with Real-time Data Visualization

Users may interact with data dynamically and intuitively because of Palantir's advances in data visualization and collaboration. The company creates interactive dashboards, scenario modeling, and real-time data exploration through the development of user-friendly user interfaces and visualization technologies. Stakeholders may successfully share insights with teams and decision-makers by using this capacity to visualize complex relationships, find correlations, and express findings. Palantir's emphasis on user-centric design improves usability and accessibility, enabling non-technical users to access and utilize complicated data.

Technologies to Strengthen Privacy

Palantir has developed privacy-enhancing solutions that prioritize data protection and regulatory compliance in response to growing concerns over data privacy and security. To protect sensitive data and reduce the danger of data breaches or unauthorized access, the company incorporates strong encryption protocols, data anonymization strategies, and access controls into its platforms. Palantir's adherence to privacy-by-design principles guarantees the security and confidentiality of client data while preserving the accuracy and usefulness of analytical procedures.

Agile Methodology and Expandability

Alex Karp

Karp highlights scalability in Palantir's technology advancements and agile development techniques. To reduce the time to market for new products and improvements, the company uses continuous deployment, fast prototyping, and iterative development cycles. Palantir's architecture is designed to be scalable to accommodate a wide range of organizations and operational complexity, including government agencies, major corporations, and startups. This allows for smooth performance optimization and integration across a variety of deployment contexts.

Solutions Tailored to Industry and Customization

Palantir is an expert at creating solutions tailored to particular industries and modifying its platforms to satisfy particular customer needs. To create tailored solutions that solve unique use cases and industry pain points, the company works closely with clients to understand sector-specific difficulties, regulatory restrictions, and commercial objectives. Palantir's adaptability and innovation ensure relevance and efficacy in tackling real-world challenges, whether in the banking, healthcare, energy, or public sector applications.

Future Directions and Thought Leadership

Palantir is still pushing the boundaries of thought leadership in the tech sector under Karp's direction, investigating cutting-edge technologies including edge computing, quantum computing, and decentralized architectures. The business makes research and development investments to investigate the possible uses of these technologies in cybersecurity, data analytics, and other fields. Palantir is positioned at the forefront of industry trends thanks to its forward-thinking approach to technology innovation, which also equips it to handle opportunities and challenges in the continuously changing digital ecosystem.

Palantir Technologies has benefited greatly from Alex Karp's leadership in creating an innovative and technologically advanced culture. Palantir keeps setting industry standards and enabling businesses with

Alex Karp

transformative data-driven solutions by advancing data integration, advanced analytics, machine learning, privacy-enhancing technology, agile development processes, and industry-specific customization. Palantir is known for being a leader in using technology to address difficult problems and promote sustainable growth in the global economy. Karp's strategic vision, dedication to technological advancement, and emphasis on ethical governance all contribute to this reputation.

Alex Karp

CHAPTER 5: LEGACY AND IMPACT

Beyond his term as CEO of Palantir Technologies, Alex Karp left a lasting legacy and shaped the company's direction and standing in the tech sector. Innovation, moral stewardship, and a dedication to using data analytics to improve society have been the hallmarks of his leadership.

Data Analytics Transformation

Palantir has revolutionized the data analytics industry by introducing cutting-edge technologies and processes, thanks to Karp's leadership. Palantir Foundry and Palantir Gotham are two of the company's platforms that have raised the bar for data integration, analysis, and visualization. Palantir's inventive methodology empowers enterprises to leverage data for enhancing

Alex Karp

operational effectiveness, formulating knowledgeable choices, and tackling intricate problems in various sectors such as banking, healthcare, energy, and defense.

Ethical Leadership and Accountability

As fundamental tenets of Palantir's operations, Karp has given ethical governance and responsibility a top priority. He has pushed for accountability, openness, and civil rights protection in the creation and application of technology. Karp is committed to promoting technical innovation while respecting societal values, and Palantir's devotion to ethical principles, such as data privacy protections and regulatory norms, reflects this commitment. Palantir has gained recognition as a reliable partner from clients, stakeholders, and regulatory authorities thanks to his emphasis on ethical leadership.

Significant Alliances and Cooperations

Palantir has developed fruitful alliances and partnerships with governmental bodies, commercial businesses, scholarly institutions, and non-profit groups under Karp's direction. These partnerships have promoted information sharing, cooperative research, and the joint creation of solutions to tackle global issues like environmental sustainability, disaster response, healthcare optimization, and national security. Palantir's collaborations broaden the company's influence and increase its reach, highlighting Karp's strategic vision of utilizing group knowledge for the good of society.

Empowerment of Governments and Organizations

With the use of Palantir's technology, governments and companies may better accomplish their strategic goals, increase operational efficiencies, and make better decisions by gaining actionable insights from complicated data environments. Palantir has been positioned by Karp's leadership as a catalyst for digital transformation, giving clients the tools they need to manage risks, seize opportunities, and navigate digital disruption in a world that is becoming more and more data-driven. Palantir's solutions have enabled a wide

Alex Karp

range of stakeholders to flourish in dynamic and competitive contexts through innovation and adaptation.

Innovative Thinking and Leadership

Among Karp's many accomplishments is Palantir's standing as a preeminent thought leader in the tech sector, spearheading innovation and influencing market patterns. Data science, AI, machine learning, and predictive analytics have advanced as a result of his emphasis on ongoing research and development. Palantir's proactive strategy equips its clients to foresee obstacles in the future and seize new possibilities, setting them up for long-term success and expansion in a digital landscape that is changing quickly.

Impact on Culture and Organization

Beyond his technical accomplishments, Karp has helped Palantir develop a culture of quality, diversity, and teamwork. Talented people dedicated to quality in service, creativity, and integrity have been nurtured

Alex Karp

under his direction. Under Karp's leadership, Palantir's open working culture promotes intellectual curiosity, innovation, and a regard for different points of view. This promotes organizational resilience and ongoing improvement.

Social responsibility and philanthropic endeavors

Palantir's dedication to corporate social responsibility and philanthropy is one of Karp's legacies. The business contributes to nonprofits, community service projects, and educational endeavors that enhance STEM education, advance social justice, and tackle global issues including public health emergencies and climate change. Palantir's charitable endeavors are a reflection of Karp's belief that technology can have a good social influence and support global sustainable development.

Prospects for the Future and Persistent Impact

Palantir is well-positioned to expand on its core values of innovation, moral leadership, and societal impact as

Alex Karp

Karp's legacy is still being lived out. The company's unwavering dedication to propelling constructive transformation and pushing the boundaries of technology is demonstrated by its persistent pursuit of excellence in data analytics, strategic alliances, and international growth. Palantir's future initiatives will be shaped by Karp's lasting influence, ensuring that the business keeps setting the standard for leadership and making significant contributions to both the IT sector and society at large.

Palantir's Worldwide Impact

Under Alex Karp's direction, Palantir Technologies has grown to be a major force in the tech sector and beyond, with a considerable worldwide impact. Palantir influences many industries and geographical areas because of its cutting-edge data analytics tools, strategic alliances, and dedication to tackling the difficult

Alex Karp

problems that face businesses, governments, and organizations all around the world.

Governmental Strategic Alliances

Palantir's strategic alliances with national and international governments have a significant impact on the company's global influence. The company's platforms—like Palantir Gotham—have proved crucial in assisting with law enforcement, disaster relief, and national security endeavors. Governments may now analyze massive volumes of data, improve situational awareness, and make data-driven choices that are vital to public safety and security thanks to Palantir's technology. Palantir's reputation as a reliable partner in governmental operations is strengthened by these collaborations, which highlight the company's role in defending individuals' rights and preserving national interests.

Sector-Specific Remedies

Alex Karp

Palantir expands its worldwide reach using industry-specific solutions that are customized to address the distinct obstacles faced by industries including finance, healthcare, energy, and manufacturing, in addition to government alliances. The business works closely with top companies to provide tailored data analytics solutions that boost productivity, stimulate innovation, and optimize business operations. Palantir's technological prowess and industry knowledge enable businesses to use data as a strategic asset, gaining an edge over competitors and sustaining growth in ever-changing market conditions.

Presence in International Markets

Palantir's extensive market presence in North America, Europe, Asia-Pacific, and the Middle East highlights the company's global significance. The business serves a wide range of clients, including government agencies, non-profits, and multinational enterprises, thanks to the maintenance of regional offices and operational hubs in strategic locations across the globe. Palantir's customized strategy makes it easier to create solutions that are specifically designed to handle local legal needs, cultural quirks, and business-specific difficulties, which increases its applicability and influence in global marketplaces.

Philanthropic and Humanitarian Projects

Palantir's dedication to charitable and humanitarian projects that tackle urgent social concerns and advance international development shows its effect on a worldwide scale. The company uses non-governmental organizations (NGOs), disaster response agencies, and humanitarian groups to work together to use its technology in emergency relief operations, crisis management, and humanitarian missions all over the world. Palantir's efforts demonstrate its ability to have a positive influence beyond business ventures by supporting humanitarian aid distribution, catastrophe planning, and data-driven decision-making in response to global disasters.

Innovative Thinking and Leadership

Alex Karp

Being a thought leader in the tech sector, Palantir has an impact on the conversation around ethical governance, AI, and data analytics on a worldwide scale. The organization actively engages in policy talks, academic conferences, and industry forums to exchange knowledge, support responsible technology usage, and influence laws that foster innovation while protecting security and privacy. Palantir's leadership in thought leadership places it at the forefront of technology innovation and best practices, shaping international standards and business trends.

Social and Cultural Impact

Palantir has a significant cultural and social impact on a worldwide scale, which is demonstrated by its diverse workplace culture, dedication to inclusion and diversity, and backing of employee-driven initiatives. The organization promotes a cooperative atmosphere that honors the many viewpoints of its workers worldwide and stimulates creativity and intellectual curiosity.

Alex Karp

Palantir's reputation as a socially conscious company that places a high priority on moral leadership, environmental sustainability, and community involvement worldwide is a result of its cultural values and social responsibility programs.

Prospects for the Future and Ongoing Growth

Looking ahead, Alex Karp's leadership of Palantir is expected to propel the company's worldwide reach higher thanks to continued innovations, strategic alliances, and a dedication to tackling changing global issues. The company will maintain its position as a disruptive force in the tech sector and strengthen its capacity to promote positive change on a global scale with its ongoing investments in R&D, market expansion, and the development of ethical governance standards. In an increasingly linked world, Palantir's lasting influence will continue to alter data analytics, technological innovation, and societal impact.

Alex Karp

Prospective Courses

Palantir Technologies' commitment to driving technological innovation, broadening its worldwide influence, and taking on challenging problems in a variety of industries is reflected in Alex Karp's vision for the company's future. Palantir is leading the way in data analytics, artificial intelligence, and ethical governance through the implementation of strategic initiatives.

Innovation in AI and Data Analytics

Palantir is committed to developing its artificial intelligence (AI) and data analytics skills going forward. The business keeps spending money on R&D to improve the sophisticated analytics tools, machine learning algorithms, and predictive modeling capabilities of its platforms, including Palantir Foundry and Gotham. Palantir can provide clients in the financial, healthcare, and defense industries with actionable insights,

Alex Karp

automated decision-making processes, and increased operational efficiency because of these breakthroughs.

Development into New Technologies

Palantir investigates new technology possibilities that could revolutionize markets and spur expansion in the years to come. This involves investigating ways to improve the speed, scalability, and security of data processing through the use of edge computing, quantum computing, and decentralized architectures. Palantir predicts future market demands and positions itself to lead innovation in data-driven solutions for global concerns by keeping at the forefront of technical breakthroughs.

Alex Karp

CONCLUSION

As we conclude our exploration of Alex Karp, the Philosopher CEO, it becomes evident that his unique blend of intellectual rigor, philosophical inquiry, and innovative leadership has profoundly shaped the trajectory of modern technology and business. Karp's journey from a scholarly background in social theory and philosophy to the helm of Palantir Technologies exemplifies the impact of interdisciplinary thinking in the corporate world.

Karp's approach to leadership is characterized by a commitment to ethical considerations and a profound understanding of the societal implications of technology. His philosophical perspective informs his decision-making, ensuring that Palantir's advancements are aligned with broader ethical and social responsibilities. This commitment is evident in Palantir's focus on developing technology that serves the public

Alex Karp

good, from combating terrorism and cyber threats to improving public health and safety.

Under Karp's leadership, Palantir has navigated complex challenges and controversies, often finding itself at the intersection of technology, politics, and ethics. Karp's ability to engage with these issues thoughtfully and transparently has reinforced his reputation as a leader who is not only driven by innovation but also guided by a deep sense of purpose and responsibility.

Karp's vision for Palantir extends beyond immediate business success. He envisions a future where technology is harnessed to address some of society's most pressing problems, fostering a more secure, transparent, and equitable world. This vision is underpinned by a belief in the power of data to drive informed decision-making and create positive change.

As we reflect on Karp's journey and contributions, it is clear that his influence extends beyond the realm of technology. His leadership philosophy, rooted in a deep understanding of human behavior and societal dynamics,

Alex Karp

offers valuable insights for leaders across industries. Karp's emphasis on ethical considerations, long-term thinking, and the broader impact of business decisions serves as a guiding principle for responsible and visionary leadership in the 21st century.

www.ingramcontent.com/pod-product-compliance
Lightning Source LLC
Chambersburg PA
CBHW071936210526
45479CB00002B/708